RIDING THROUGH THE DOWNERS, HASSLES, SNAGS AND FUNKS

RIDING
THROUGH THE
DOWNERS,
HASSLES,
SNAGS
AND FUNKS

Ari Kiev, M.D.

E. P. DUTTON · NEW YORK

For information contact: Elsevier-Dutton
Publishing Co., Inc.,
2 Park Avenue, New York, N.Y. 10016

Library of Congress Cataloging in Publication Data

Kiev, Ari.
    Riding through the downers, hassles, snags and funks.
    1. Depression, Mental.   2. Adolescent psychology.
I. Title.
RJ506.D4K53   1980   616.85′27   80-15678

ISBN: 0-525-93138-4

Published simultaneously in Canada by Clarke, Irwin &
Company Limited, Toronto and Vancouver

10   9   8   7   6   5   4   3   2   1

First Edition

RIDING THROUGH THE DOWNERS, HASSLES, SNAGS AND FUNKS

I

Dear Friend,

Thanks for your very expressive letter. I can see how isolated and lonely you're feeling, but if you'll bear with me for a little while I think I can help you find a way out of the "mess" you describe, or at least show you some light at the end of the tunnel. Don't worry, I know you don't want to hear how wonderful life is or how much you have to live for. I'm not going to preach to you.

You say you've been feeling depressed for some time, and at this point you can't even remember how it started. You're feeling "overwhelmed" and even the most routine tasks are more than you can manage. You have trouble making decisions and no matter which ones you make, they always seem to be wrong. You're frustrated, dejected and angry. No matter what you do, you can't seem to feel anything but down.

Those are pretty hard feelings to live with, and I'm not surprised that you've been trying to bury them by pretending they don't exist. It's clear you don't feel very good, but from what you say it seems as if you're acting just the opposite. Bad as you feel inside, you do what's expected of you with a stiff smile; like somebody constantly on stage, you keep your true emotions hidden.

On the surface your acting seems to be working. Most people don't recognize your inner turmoil, and so you're successfully avoiding a lot of questions, conflicts and complaints. But you're using an enormous amount of energy to do this, and that energy is being subtracted from other areas of your life. Because you're working so hard at your disguise, you don't have time for much else. No wonder you're just "not interested" any more in things that used to please you.

Now, holding in feelings the way you're doing can really tie you up in knots. This is because it is very difficult to function as if you feel normal and strong when in fact you feel terrible. Feeling terrible and disguising it means that a lot of the time you're angry with *yourself* as well as with other people, because you're constantly refusing to stand up for the way you really feel. For many people, hiding "bad" feelings leads to resentment and guilt at not being genuine, and this in turn can intensify a depression.

Most of us talk about "being depressed" or "feeling blue" from time to time. But it doesn't sound to me as if that's how you're feeling. Your depression seems much more long-range than a momentary down. In fact you sound so consumed with despair and so hopeless about the chances of improving your life that I can well understand why you feel at times there's no point in going on.

I know a long-term depression can be a pretty awful thing, because its specific symptoms, both physical and psychological, seem to nourish your feelings of despair. You wake up too early in the morning after sleeping fitfully the night before. You've lost interest in food. You have no energy. Your arms and legs feel heavy. You suffer from headaches. You have feelings of dread which paralyze you when you get up, then mysteriously disappear sometime in the afternoon. You worry about school, and because you worry you can't concentrate, and that makes you worry more.

You've felt this way for months, and you've begun to feel alienated and reluctant to assume responsibility or follow any routine. You have trouble expressing yourself or asserting your point of view. You feel unappreciated, unloved, even worthless. External pressures, which seem overwhelming, make you angry, yet you are convinced you shouldn't feel that way and that you are strange or sick because you do. You're afraid to get angry with people you feel are pressuring you because you might explode, go to pieces or clobber someone. As bad as you feel, you're most afraid of losing control and doing something that will make you feel even more guilty.

To top it off, you feel trapped in a situation you cannot change that is making you feel helpless. You feel your depression will never end, that no one will ever understand you, and that it's useless to try to do anything about it.

You may feel your entire life—even your own body—is out of your control. You may get the feeling that you are standing outside of your body watching yourself go through the motions of being alive—as if you were strapped into a chair watching yourself on TV. This is a common occurrence in depression. It's what we call a "defense mechanism": a way that your mind turns off feelings of intolerable frustration by convincing you that the whole thing is out of your hands. If you don't understand how such a mechanism works, you can be very frightened by it, since it leaves you feeling that nothing is real and that your mind is separate from your body. This explains the feeling of numbness you describe which has led you to want to cut yourself to see if you'd bleed. No wonder you say you are afraid of "losing your mind."

You say too that you can't relate to others any more; a thick, invisible glass wall seems to divide you from everybody you know, and gives you the feeling of being trapped inside your own body. Paradoxically, at the same time everybody seems to be pushing you to do this or do that, to be this way or that way; nobody leaves you enough elbow room to do what *you* want to do. And since you're not at all sure yourself what that is, you're an easy mark for unsolicited suggestions, advice and "help."

Worst of all, you're preoccupied with recurring morbid thoughts, in addition to an extreme sense of guilt about your apparent inability to act. The same images keep jamming your head, coming back over and over again, until all you want to do is to get rid of them. You feel like hitting your head against the wall or jumping out of the window. Thoughts of suicide rise up. You push them down, but they keep returning. You don't want to die, but sometimes you feel as if that would be better than putting up with your own troubled mind. Horrifying as it seems to you, suicide looks sometimes like the only way to rid yourself of your intolerable tensions.

This is the way that most depressions feel, and the fact that, as you say, you've been feeling this kind of tension for several months means that, like many other depressed people, you're caught in a vicious circle. Not only do you feel bad, but you feel bad *about* feeling bad; the longer the cycle of depression-anger-depression goes on, the worse you feel for letting it go on, and the more intolerant of yourself you become. It doesn't help a bit to know that other people have felt, and are still feeling, the same way, because you are locked firmly into your own situation. Far from being reassured by knowing that depression is common, you feel surrounded by a wall of darkness, an impenetrable barrier which prevents you from reaching out to other people.

Because of this, I know how hard it was for you to write to me, and I am glad you found the courage to do so.

Right now you probably feel utterly pessimistic about the chances of anyone else—a parent, a friend or a doctor—being able to help you through the nightmare. I know that you must often feel there is no one who really cares about you, who has a handle on your inner torture. Your parents, like most parents, are probably not very good listeners. They are feeling guilty about you, but they don't know how to break through the wall around you. Instead of listening, they preach. They may mean well, but their advice usually comes down to a facile admonition to snap out of it and get down to work. Which only makes you feel worse. Their puritanical, common sense approach to your difficulties might work fine under ordinary circumstances, but when you're depressed it's exactly the wrong approach.

At other times your parents may seem as solicitous and sweet as they are generally harsh and demanding. Trying to overcompensate for being too rough on you, they may sometimes go out of their way to do you little favors, to make your favorite foods, to buy you unexpected presents and generally to protect you by kindness from the trouble you are carrying inside. Naturally this is no more helpful than their demands; it only makes you feel like an overgrown grade-schooler, more helpless than ever before.

Your friends are not much better. They too may mean well when they brush off your problems as insignificant, when they say, "Come on, forget it. Let's go to a movie." But they are really no more in touch with your true feelings of fear and resentment than your parents. Their demands that you look on the bright side only reinforce your conviction that they cannot, or will not, penetrate your invisible wall.

Now, I promised I wouldn't preach to you, and I won't. But you have to allow me one brief observation that may put all the good intentions of those around you in perspective. It's the first thing you'll have to keep in mind if you want to get to that light at the end of the tunnel: the startlingly simple fact that you, and only you, can really say how you are feeling and what you should be doing about it. No one else can ever fully comprehend your feelings. It is important to remember this when others try to be helpful, for in their eagerness they sometimes unwittingly involve you in obligations that can actually escalate, rather than diminish, your problems. In trying to live up to their expectations of you, you can end up feeling worse than ever. In trying to keep your mind, as they advise, on the bright side, you may simply come to realize the truth of Tennyson's observation that "sorrow's crown of sorrow is remembering happier things."

That is why, against all the dictates of common sense, I hope that you ignore the urgings of others that you get moving again, and predictions that everything will be all right as soon as you take charge of your life. Sure, adversity can be overcome through effort—but not when your energy is down. Sure, great things can be accomplished by will-power—but not when you're depressed. The simplistic idea that you should "keep going" to overcome your depression is just not good advice; in fact, the harder you push yourself to function normally when you're depressed, the more likely you are to end up feeling worse. You're already being hard enough on yourself, after all. It's not a wise course to add to your feelings of resentment and frustration by forcing yourself to do things you just don't feel up to.

Like most depressed people, you seem to be giving yourself a pretty hard time. Maybe if I tell you some of the basic facts we know about depression, you might see why you should let up on yourself a little bit.

First of all, depressions—yours or anyone else's—are not due to a lack of willpower. Nor are they a result of laziness. You are not goofing off when you can't get up in the morning, and you're not faking it or looking for sympathy when you can't sleep or can't make a decision. You must understand what those around you too often forget: that you don't *want* to feel depressed, or to experience the distress of insomnia, energy loss and fear. If you are experiencing these things, it does not mean you are a moral or physical coward.

As far as doctors now know, depression is the result of certain physiological responses to stress to which some people are more predisposed than others. That's all. It's not a curse or an irreversible condition or a cross you must bear forever. It's a physical and mental phenomenon that can be treated successfully with specific medicines. These anti-depressant or "mood elevating" medications correct the reduction in the levels of nerve transmitters in the central nervous system that is part of the physiological response to stress. The medicines have none of the potential for addiction that alcohol and street drugs have, and they relieve the symptoms of depression simply and rapidly. Medication may also prove especially helpful in breaking up self-cycling patterns of anxiety which may be adding to your distress.

I'm not trying to convince you to visit your doctor (who can prescribe such medicines) or even to see a psychiatrist. I simply want you to know that specific medical relief is available if your symptoms persist too long. Whether you opt for this course of action or you decide to ride through the depression on your own you should know that it can be dealt with.

If it couldn't be dealt with, human history would have been very different. Abraham Lincoln, Nathaniel Hawthorne, Winston Churchill, astronaut Buzz Aldrin and Sigmund Freud, to name only a few accomplished people, all had recurrent bouts of depression. Churchill even had a name for his. He called it "my black dog." So you're not exactly in bad company.

All of these people managed to ride through or work through their depressions, and that points to a crucial fact about the disorder: no depression lasts forever. Whether you are treated medically or not, your depression will eventually come to an end.

You may already have a hint of this, if your depression is of the "mood-swing" variety. No doubt you're familiar with the daily rises and falls in feeling that most of us call our "ups and downs." For depressed people, these ups and downs seem much more intense, and yet they are quite typical of the condition. Invariably mornings are the worst time of day (this reflects internal biological mechanisms), and fighting extra hard to get up and get going may therefore be a hopeless and inevitably frustrating experience. One of the first steps in combating depression, therefore, is understanding not only the temporary character of the "down" state but also its reality.

What *should* you do when you're depressed? Well, if you had a broken leg, you wouldn't expect to jog two miles a day or keep going to football practice while it mended. You'd stay off your feet for a while and take it easy. If you were running a high fever, you wouldn't jump in a pool and start doing laps. You'd get in bed and rest until you were better. Essentially you should use the same kind of caution when you're feeling down. Don't push yourself, but find a level of activity at which you can comfortably function.

If you're feeling so bad that you don't want to

get out of bed to face the day, stay there. Take it easy for a while; a brief time out from your responsibilities can be beneficial, in spite of what seems like common sense. It makes more sense to treat yourself like a patient than to force yourself to perform when you can't. "While grief is fresh," said Samuel Johnson, "every attempt to divert only irritates. You must wait till it be digested, and then amusement will dissipate the remains."

Now, nobody is going to understand this. It runs counter to everything you've been told up to now, by your parents, your friends, perhaps even your doctors. Your parents especially are likely to have trouble with the suggestion that you take it easy for a while, because they have such high hopes for you, and these cannot be realized by staying in bed. I know it's hard to resist them, and to resist feeling guilty for disappointing them. But remember that only you can decide when you're ready to get up and face the world. Remember that disguising your feelings of helplessness by mock bravado can actually intensify them, while giving in for a time to the way you feel can gradually release the pressure and make you feel less tense.

Doing this, of course, means taking your problem seriously even though those around you may not be willing to do so. People who try to comfort depressed children or friends often minimize, and sometimes even ignore, what is going on under their noses. They may attribute your difficulties to the changes of adolescence, or explain your loss of interest in school as merely temporary and unimportant, even normal for your age. Yet you know (probably better than your parents) that not all adolescents feel depressed, and you sense, even if you cannot put it into words, that what is troubling you is something more serious than just a passing stage of growth. If your loss of initiative, your inefficiency, your listlessness and the other problems you describe are taken as normal occurrences for your age, your chances of overcoming them will be greatly reduced. You can overcome them, as I hope to show you, but first you must recognize them as unique, serious and real.

But recognizing that you have a problem is only the beginning. Next you must find a way to overcome it. I hope you will take my advice, and take that short breather first: relax and take a slow, hard look at the invisible wall around you. Then stay with me while I see if I can show you a way to surmount it.

II

Useful as it may be for you to sit back and relax for a while, eventually you're going to need to get out of bed, confront the wall around you and get your life moving again. I know this isn't easy. Once you've relaxed—once you've gotten used to inactivity—the natural tendency is to let it take over. The force that physicists call inertia—the force that keeps moving objects moving and stopped objects at rest—frequently proves of greater power than anybody's purpose or will.

When you're depressed, inertia has a real edge on you, because along with the guilt and resentment, you often have a heightened awareness of the absurdity of life, which makes you wonder if there's any point in going on. Since no one is connecting with you, the attempt to make sense of your life can seem pointless and unreal.

This feeling of rejection and emptiness, the sense of futility that is sometimes called existential despair, comes over every one of us at one time or another. It may be of some use to you, as you sit there wondering how to begin, to learn where the feeling originates.

Essentially feelings of rejection arise as a result of the progressively decreasing support we get from our parents, and later our friends, as we grow older. When we're infants, pretty much everything we do is applauded. As we grow, however, we're obliged to learn certain appropriate ways of doing things, and to avoid others. When you were young your parents probably very often showed you the right way to perform certain tasks, and although this was meant to help you, it also implied that the way you were doing it was wrong—and that you were wrong as well. Most of us have this experience as children, and as a result, at the root of our sense of self is some feeling about not being "OK."

From your description of your parents, it sounds like they took your strengths for granted when you were younger, and focused attention on your weaknesses so you could become stronger. This has left you with some residue of bad feelings about yourself. Such feelings can make you feel inadequate, unloved and unlovable. Even though we all learn to cover up such recognitions of our own fallibility, we understand they are there. As we learn to behave in socially acceptable ways, we sense that those who respond to our social side are ignoring our negative side, and as a result we never feel fully accepted.

I suspect this is why you feel so isolated. Because you fear being rejected or ridiculed for your secret "negative" side, you communicate in roundabout ways. In addition you're not exactly sure what you want to communicate, and you frequently fail to comprehend what others are trying to say—what they want or need. Just as you're beginning to assert your identity in relation to others, you are becoming painfully aware of the complex connection between thought and language, and beginning to see how complicated communication can be.

Yet some of your anxiety may be unrealistic. Like most of us, you may be misperceiving the intentions and expectations of other people, suspecting ill will or deviousness where none exists. So aware are you that you are a secret sinner that you imagine everyone else must be aware of this too.

But the problem is more than mere misperception, because on top of this you've no doubt been experiencing actual, tangible evidence that you are a failure or worthless. Even if until now you've always been at the top of the heap, slowly but surely this situation is beginning to end. As you note, you are going through a lot of changes, and have experienced a number of real rejections. First of all you didn't make the college of your choice. Then your first romance came to an abrupt halt for reasons that were never clear to you. Finally, your parents grounded you for two weeks because your attitude at school was negative.

In the midst of all this rejection, it's not surprising that you're often disconsolate and confused. It's not surprising either that you see the requests and suggestions of others not as honest offers of help, but as badgering, nagging demands. At this point in your life, you are simply facing too many choices. No wonder you are having trouble in knowing whose values to follow, and even in knowing what all those outside voices want of you. Your inclination is to try to meet your parents' demands, but are you perceiving them correctly? You wonder sometimes how they can have your best interests at heart when they are so inclined to pressure you—and this makes you buck them just for spite.

But it's not just your parents. You haven't learned to say no to the demands of your friends either—demands that often conflict with your parents' (not to mention your own) expectations. You're tired of having others tell you what to do, but you're not confident enough yet to be able to tell yourself. And you don't want to alienate people, because that would make the wall thicker than it already is.

Adolescence is never an easy time. It's the first time in your life when you are faced with the challenge of setting goals for your future, so the decisions you have to make are huge. If you lack a set of personal goals, if you have too many goals, or if your goals are challenging or confusing, you can feel considerable anxiety no matter how good your choices look. The mere range of those choices can be truly bewildering, I know, and unfortunately, I can't give you a neat prescription to make your decisions easier.

I can, however, tell you something very important about the need for goals in general. Even though inertia may be in charge now, selecting *some* goal—even if you aren't sure of your preferences—will help you to get moving sooner. The important thing is to have an object, no matter which one, to move towards. This is because changes are always easier to manage when you are in motion than when you are stalled. Remember that inertia can work for you as well as against you; sometimes that initial decision just to get out of bed and take a walk can be the most decisive factor.

What kind of goal should you set? That's up to you, of course, but I'd strongly suggest that you not aim for the stars just yet. If you were a runner just getting over a case of the flu, you wouldn't start the first day back at practice trying to break the four-minute mile. You'd start slowly, and work up to the bigger achievements.

Disappointment can come, moreover, not only by aiming too high, but by scattering your shot too wide. Making too many commitments, especially to activities which are only of marginal interest to you, can cause resentment and ultimately more depression. A failure to focus on one goal at a time may lead to an excessive preoccupation with results and a search for applause, and in the long run this too can increase your suffering.

In other words, don't try out for the cheering squad or take up the guitar, simply because they seem like popular or hip things to do. Choose what you want to do, and what is within your reach, rather than follow someone else's conventional idea of success. You know best what interests you. If you insist on pursuing someone else's dream, you're really only buying into a nightmare. Without even knowing your specific interests, I can tell from your letter that some of your distress is a result of the fact that until now you have been pursuing goals set for you by your parents, rather than those you have set for yourself.

You say that pressures are coming at you from all sides. No matter how hard you try, they just don't let up. When you think you've got one problem licked, another one rears its head. Like the John Wayne character in *The Shootist*, just as you've sized up the guy in front of you, you're nailed by somebody who's snuck in the back door with a shotgun.

I know that feeling of being surrounded can be frightening, but when you think about it, you know it will pass in time, or at least become less significant. Some of the distress you feel is like the "pregame jitters" or the "butterflies" most of us get just before a race or a speech. Some of this results from uncertainty and the unfamiliarity of the situation; some of it results from excessive efforts to eliminate the tension—which can actually create more of it. Once you learn how to flow with your anxiety rather than eliminate it, you will see that your distress is not going to last forever, and you will feel more comfortable and be better able to cope with your pressures. If in addition you can stop doing the things which intensify your distress, it will pass much quicker. In this connection I would remind you that a lot of your negative thoughts come from bottled-up feelings (especially angry feelings) which you are reluctant to express except, self-destructively, toward yourself. Your self-destructive thoughts really reflect your suppressed desire to assert yourself, and to the extent that you can learn to express anger externally, you will become less self-destructive and more self-creative.

Again, I don't say this is easy. Not only is it

difficult to set reasonable, single-minded goals, but there is no guarantee once you do set them that the first one, or the tenth, will be realized the way you want. If you keep at it, though, you will achieve a goal, and will then be able to see your present suffering as so much preparation for that end.

What Lord Byron said is quite true: "Sorrows are our best educators. A man can see further through a tear than a telescope." That may be cold comfort to you now, but don't dismiss it entirely. I don't want to romanticize depression, because we both know it's not very glamorous, but if it can be said to have a virtue it's that it usually leads to growth. "Out of suffering," said E. H. Chapin, "emerge the strongest souls." By going through these difficult times now, you will gain greater self-awareness and develop a firmer sense of your own identity.

Sooner or later everyone has got to recognize his limits, to accept himself and begin to live life as it was meant to be lived—independently, not pseudo-independently. The earlier you can discover this, the sooner you will discover your own unique potential and begin to assume responsibility for yourself. This is difficult because giving up your comfortable, outer self in order to reveal the turbulent, interesting, inner self can be very threatening. But this is the task of adolescence.

All through life you are going to be faced with decisions, with opportunities to define your identity and take a stand on issues. From the angry tone of your letter, I suspect that, like most of us at one time or another, you want to do this but are holding back out of a fear of failure or ridicule. Even when you have felt overworked, you have been unable to ask for help. Sometimes you know what you want but can't bring yourself to request it. Consciously or unconsciously you maneuver others into sharing decisions with you because of a fear that you will be judged as too aggressive if you make them for yourself. In trying to deny your true feelings, however, you generate enormous stress and in the end make poor decisions: this is why no matter what you decide, it always seems to be wrong. If you can start to make decisions without worrying what others will think of them, you will be on the road to defining yourself rather than have others tell you who you are. And isn't that what you really want to do?

I think too that you are afraid to let yourself feel good: afraid others will reject you for taking something (happiness) that you don't believe you deserve. You may even search out situations where you can be seen suffering to avoid having to face the fact that you secretly don't want to be happy.

How do you change this state of affairs?

You can begin by looking at your present situation as a turning point of your life—a moment when you can take the first steps towards leading a life in accord with your own unique desires. You may think you've come to the end of the line, but there is nothing objectively accurate about that assessment: it's a subjective judgment you can change. If you can begin to look closely at important problems in your life and try to start solving them in accord with your own, and not others', needs, then your depression will begin to lift, and you will learn to function productively in spite of the unavoidable stresses of daily life.

Later I'll give you some specific hints as to how to go about this. Now I'll just ask you to remember that life is a marathon, not a sprint. If no one has ever explained this to you, it's easy to think of yourself as a failure. But the journey is in front of you, not behind. Yesterday's results are history. If you were to believe at this point in your life that you were a success and could rest on your laurels, in fact, you'd be in far worse shape than one who has failed, since you would then stop growing and learning. The real key to success is resilience, the ability to bounce back from failure. Working with Olympic athletes for a number of years, I found repeatedly that the distinguishing mark of the real champions, the Muhammad Alis of the world, was their lack of a fear of failure. In fact, champions are stimulated by their failures. They learn from them how to go on with the race, at the same time that they learn not to be distracted by their successes.

You may already have failed at a number of things. You may even believe that life has passed you by, and that there is no way you can make things work out right. That's an understandable but false perception. The truth is that you were simply unprepared for discouragements and setbacks which could have happened to anyone. If you can visualize your life as a long-distance run, one for which you are continually revising your strategy, you can begin to think—and to behave—like a winner. Nobody tallies up all victories and no defeats; the successes are the people who learn from the latter and go on.

What I am suggesting is that you can write your own script, and that this can help you become whatever you want to be. Can you become chairman of the board, a Pulitzer Prize winner, an Olympic medalist? Maybe, and maybe not. But you will only know if you begin by picking an attainable goal and beginning; the goal itself is unimportant, but marshalling your now dormant energies to choose one is. The day you pick a specific goal and start working toward it, you will begin to control your life.

It has taken me a long time to recognize the simple truth that the effort to reach a goal is more important than the goal itself. The virtue of goals is largely to challenge you, to bring out your best, to give you perspective and direction. Achieving the goal is not critical, though it can certainly be pleasant and rewarding. I emphasize this because you sound defeated about not achieving certain goals, mistakenly assuming that they are critical for your peace of mind when in fact they are only signposts to a yet unwritten future.

Ultimately, satisfaction comes from making the most of your own specific talents and capacities. Duplicating what others have done can never give you the gratification that developing your own interests can. But since no one can tell you which is your best choice, you must be willing to try a variety of activities until you find one that clicks for you.

When you take a journey, you keep moving, trying to cover as much territory as possible. Each day you get up early in anticipation of new sights, sounds, smells and experiences. Some days are good and some are rotten, but each one offers new opportunities, and if you keep moving you are bound to have some good times along the way. In addition, the more you travel, the better you get at it. You learn how to handle foreign currencies without getting ripped off. You learn where to drink the water and where not to. You learn what kinds of sites turn you on and which ones you'd just as soon avoid. When I first began traveling, I always went to the recommended places, the "right" spots on the map. But as I continued I found more and more that the places I was supposed to go just didn't interest me, so I gradually learned to revise my itinerary, to make my own markings on the map. Now I plan my trips with me in mind, and leave the tours to the neophytes.

Of course, to plot your traveling—or your life—this way, you have to be willing to look around, to try new approaches, to invent. Last year I was stuck on a train to the ancient Incan city of Machu Picchu for seven hours because I explored only the conventional possibility. Seven hours on a train to spend one hour at the ruins! Only when I got back from that grueling experience did I discover that I could have had a thirty-minute helicopter ride instead and taken aerial shots of the whole site besides. No one had told me there were helicopters, and I never bothered to investigate.

Perhaps no one has told you there are helicopters either. Perhaps no one has ever told you that you were on a journey, or that, with practice, you could improve the quality of that journey. But to do this, you have to start small.

Even Sir Edmund Hillary, one of the first men up Mt. Everest, began with smaller mountains, and went through training and considerable hardship before conquering the "roof of the world." The same principles that governed his preparation apply to the kinds of overwhelming experiences you are having right now. Because you haven't been trained to deal with them, you are uncomfortable with your reactions, fearful of dealing with the unknown and wary of tapping yourself rather than

others for advice. With exercise, patience and per-
severance, all of that can change. I don't say you'll
be able to scale a Himalayan peak tomorrow, but
just taking that first step, that first walk outside to
look around, is a healthy start.

From there you can look into helicopters.

Most of us are brought up to believe that everything
in our lives must happen naturally and that to consciously plan how to behave or to respond to a situation is somehow manipulative or insincere. Nothing
could be further from the truth. In fact few of us
have the capacity, as the Beatles song put it, to
"act naturally"; to expect that going with your feelings will make everything come out fine is just wishful thinking. For one thing, your feelings are not
simple and clear-cut—as you already know. For
another, it often takes a great deal of conscious effort to figure out which of your many con-
flicting emotions are the real ones in any given
situation.

So even though I've said that you'd be better off
if you learn to express your feelings rather than
conceal them, I'm well aware that finding out what
those feelings are can be a major task in itself. You
can get your emotions and your thoughts under
control, but it's not simply a matter of recognizing
the real you and taking it from there. In a sense

there is no real you; you are what you make of yourself each day.

Basically, deciding what to think about or how to cope with different situations is a matter of recognizing that your brain—no less than your arm or the way you comb your hair—is under your control. You can decide what you're going to think about, and the way in which you're going to function. Leaving these processes to chance or to random impulses means giving up the right to use your intellectual and emotional gifts for your own good. Going with the flow, in other words, can be a quick way of doing yourself in. Learning how to choose what to think about so you can control your responses, on the other hand, can give you a sense of real confidence and keep you from being overwhelmed by the pressures around you.

It can also be a way of effecting change not only in yourself, but in those around you. Remember that the only person you can change directly is you. But if you change your own behavior, you'll find that others will automatically begin to react differently to you, and this means, in effect, that you will have changed them as well.

You say you feel trapped in your situation and cannot seem to change it. You feel you have no free choice, free time or free will, but are constantly being controlled by others.

That's a common and understandable feeling—but it's the result of an erroneous assumption: that other people have power over you even if you don't want them to. That is simply wrong. You *can* keep the world from stepping on your toes, and the way you begin is simply by controlling your own behavior. You can set limits on the extent to which you cooperate with other people's demands, spoken or silent. And you don't have to be a hermit in a forest. You can set limits no matter how intimately or constantly you are involved with others.

How do you do it? Well, to begin with, the more you control the smallest, most insignificant actions of your daily life, the less chance there will be of tension and depression building up within you, and subsequently the more control you will have. You *can* reduce the stress and tension in your life, but you've got to start small.

Take an example. When the Apollo astronauts were training for the moon shots, they knew that they would soon be subjected to levels of stress that few people in human history had ever experienced. No doubt that gave them many shaky moments. But they didn't deal with the problem, at the beginning, head on. That is, they didn't train specifically to confront the overpowering tension of lift-off or reentry or landing. What they did was to prepare themselves, physically and emotionally, in small ways. They learned to note when their blood pressure and breathing were abnormal, and they learned to become calm in the face of that. They learned to observe and then, gradually, to control the many physiological reactions that even minor stress elicits—so that by the time the real test came, they were ready. At lift-off their blood pressure and pulse rates were exceptionally high, but because of their training, they came through the mission splendidly. Because practice had taught them what was coming, they didn't panic: they were dealing, after all, with an unruly but well-known friend—their own stress responses.

If you learn first to observe your own stress

responses as they did, you can then learn how to control how you react to them. Take a spot check of yourself. The next time your parents yell at you or you feel neglected at a party, ask yourself, "How is my body feeling about this? Are my palms sweaty? Do I feel unusually hot or cold? Is my heartbeat normal or fast? How does my stomach feel?" Getting in touch with the basic physiological symptoms of stress can be a valuable prelude to assessing how to deal with them. If you can't even feel that your stomach is doing flips, you won't have a very good chance of getting it to slow down.

After self-observation, the important next step is self-control. "He who reigns within himself and rules his passions, desires, and fears," said the English poet John Milton, "is more than a king." The person who can learn to calm himself in the midst of misfortune or nervousness has a far better chance of success in all areas of life than the one who is prey to a thousand tricks and turns of emotion. This takes a bit of training and practice, to be sure, but any effort toward that end will be well worth your trouble.

I don't mean that you should lie to yourself or to others, pretending to be calm when you're not. In fact, that's just the opposite of what you want to do. What I mean is that, faced with a troubling or threatening situation, you should strive for balance and poise; you should hold off a bit before you lash out at someone who has offended you; you should think before either responding in anger, or retreating in sullenness; you should have enough confidence in your own sensibilities to temper your anxiety with reason, knowing that that can only bring clarity and patience into your view of the situation.

The tragedy, and the beauty, of human consciousness is, as the American poet Wallace Stevens said, that "We live in the mind." Many of us take this knowledge as a kind of curse, and feel that we are doomed to be imprisoned in our own heads. But it need not be that way. Understanding the primacy of subjective consciousness can, in fact, be a step on the road to psychological freedom, for if your thoughts determine both your behavior and the circumstances and events around you, then you can actually influence the kinds of experiences you have in the world, by learning to program and select your thoughts.

Maybe you think this is all nonsense. Maybe it doesn't explain the facts as you know them: the fact, for example, that the brain of your class has been getting straight A's since the first grade with no effort at all, or that others, no matter how hard they seem to work, are still flunking chemistry or English. You may even feel that no matter how hard you try, you still won't be able to do what others are doing without effort.

Well, that may be true, but so what? The point is to discover what you do well, not to follow somebody else's footsteps or plans. And everybody does something well. It may take a little looking, but you can find it. Only you won't find it very fast if you start out thinking you can't.

Approaching things from a negative viewpoint, in other words, is like giving yourself two strikes before you even step up to the plate. The batter who enters the box convinced he can't do anything against the pitcher's famous curve will very likely end up striking out. This is an example of what we call a self-fulfilling prophecy: the person who constantly predicts defeat for himself often ends up, not surprisingly, in last place; while the person who habitually predicts success has a far greater chance of achieving it.

You say you are reluctant to act because of a fear of failing. Sure. I understand that. We're all afraid of blowing it, of looking like fools in front of our friends. But why not consider a different viewpoint? Maybe it's precisely your unwillingness to act which insures your continued failures. Maybe you've got the whole thing backwards, and the only reason success has eluded you is that you've denied yourself that 100 percent effort that would bring it within your reach.

When you focus all of your energy on the task before you, and waste none of it thinking about the outcome, you achieve unexpectedly gratifying results. In many endeavors such spectacular results come only after you have pushed yourself beyond where you thought you could go. Like the marathon runner who gets a "second wind" just when he or she thought it was all over, you may find that success is simply a matter of a little extra try.

Most of us who fear failure do so out of an unnecessarily strong sense of defensiveness: since we don't want people to laugh at us, we refuse to put ourselves in any situations where that might be a possible outcome. But by depriving ourselves of the chance to fail, we also deprive ourselves of the chance to succeed, and we end up risking—and doing—nothing rather than risk anything at all. This puts us in a perpetual limbo.

You can gain valuable perspective on yourself from failure if you control your defensiveness. This means getting into the habit of tolerating uncomfortable situations and feelings, and at the same time refusing to blame other people for your discomfort. Most of us, when we feel down, look outside ourselves for a reason. Talking about bad feelings then becomes an exercise not in expression, but in attack. If we're feeling lousy, we say to ourselves that somebody else (never ourselves) must be at fault.

You can see how destructive this can be to yourself. To counter the effects of this kind of bad habit—and it's a habit we all have—I employ a role-playing exercise in my Life Strategy Workshops. You tell someone else how you feel without putting them—or yourself—on the defensive. This is harder than it sounds, but with practice it is possible to talk about your feelings without trying to justify them or attribute them to the person with whom you are talking.

Say, for example, that a friend has just dismissed your opinion of a new movie with the comment, "I think you missed the real point." Your first inclination might be to snap back: "That really ticks me off. What the hell do you know about it, anyway?" Yet this would be merely another heated opinion, and obviously would only close off further conversation. A better approach might be to tell your friend just how his or her abrupt dismissal made you feel. "I feel uncomfortable and angry with that idea, and think I'll be better off if we can postpone this discussion," you might say. "My head is pulsating, my arms are tense, and I have a gnawing sensation in the pit of my stomach. Do you ever feel this way?"

The first reaction is a defensive, automatic response designed to make yourself look better than the antagonist. The second reaction is a conscious attempt, however pained, to communicate, an open admission of your own vulnerability. You may not believe that your efforts to express yourself straightforwardly like this can make a difference, or that hostile reactions generally only trigger more hostile ones. I know it's easy to think that you can be happy only if you are right and someone else is wrong. But if you are to find your own way, you must set yourself beyond comparisons. Naturally if you spend your time constantly comparing what you have with what someone else has, or what you have achieved with someone else's accomplishments, you're going to be miserable. The medals are always shinier on someone else's chest. You want to strive for a situation in which you determine your own failures and successes, in which you use your own particular assets to the fullest measure possible, and in which your view of yourself is not contingent on anybody' else's view of you.

You don't have to prove yourself to anybody. The sooner you realize this, the better you will begin to feel.

What I'm getting at, I guess, is that changing your present circumstances is a matter of concentrating on efforts rather than results. Since we're pretty much obsessed with results, with performance, in our culture, that's often very difficult. But it's the only path I know to freedom, to the freedom that comes when you know that you are the one calling the shots.

I know it's easy to get discouraged. But, after all, everybody loses. "The best laid plans of mice and men," said the Scottish poet Robert Burns, "gang aft aglay." So you can never count on success.

What you can count on is your own ability to withstand things, no matter what the outcome. Developing the ability to roll with the punches, to laugh at yourself, to approach winning and losing philosophically rather than as a matter of life and death—these things in the long run will serve you far better than a perfect foul-shot record or an 800 on your college boards.

You can, however, maximize your chances of success by paying attention to another important aspect of change; that is, that most of us live most of our lives by rote, but that it is possible to alter this by conscious preparation and planning. We may be creatures of habit, but no habit is unbreakable, and ultimately the critical issue for your happiness is your ability to shift out of your habitual patterns of response into a pattern that brings you greater joy, greater opportunity for expression. To do this, you have to be able to visualize your habitual responses in advance, and become especially aware of those kinds of situations which trigger a habitually anxious response.

From what you say, you are commonly anxious when you accede to the requests of others in order not to offend them or make them angry with you—even though you know you are acting contrary to your best interests. Well, since you know this kind of situation almost always makes you uptight, why not plan for it in advance right now? Tell yourself that the next time this kind of thing comes up, you're going to do something different. You're not simply going to sit through it and suffer.

Say, for example, that you hate listening to a certain long-winded friend on the telephone, but have done so uncomplainingly in the past for fear of offending him. While it might not make things any easier for you to tell him, "Look, Joe, I think you're a bore and I wish you'd shut up," it will help if you begin by making a small change in the way you respond to the situation. You don't have to offend him, but you can make yourself feel differently about what is going on. Try, for example, to write down notes of what your windy friend says. It may not make him any less wordy, but it will make what he says less oppressive to you, because writing it down will act as a distancing factor. In addition, you'll have something concrete to reflect on when you review the conversation with yourself later: your notes could give you some insight into your own responses and into why, specifically, you feel put-upon whenever that particular friend calls. With that as a basis, you can ease into telling him to slow down.

It's a curious paradox, but changes in behavior often precede, rather than follow, internal change. That is, by altering an external habit you may find that you have also altered the internal responses, the agitation and stress, you have habitually associated with it. The philosopher William James, for example, was convinced that literally "whistling in the dark" could actually make someone less fearful of the dark. Far from being an act of false bravado, putting up a display of courage, in James's estimation, frequently led to the whistler's actually feeling more courageous.

Remember that when you are asked to do something you just don't want to do, you always have the option of doing something else instead. And you can do this right now, right while the external circumstances of your life are exactly the same as they have always been. It's simply chasing phantoms to believe that everything will be all right as soon as you've dropped out of school, gotten married, moved to San Francisco, told off your teachers or parents, or gone into debt for a new car. They won't be. The only thing that can make them all right is your decision to change the way you react to the situations, good and bad, in which you find yourself.

That decision, of course, is only an initial step. Beyond that, you have to begin to set goals for yourself, and move consciously and with determination to carry them out.

IV

In recent years people in the human potential movement have been talking about "finding their centers," or "becoming centered" as a way of achieving greater happiness and self-esteem. What they mean by being centered is being so in touch with your own needs and desires that the opinions and urgings of others do not affect you adversely. You've found your own center of gravity, as it were, so like one of those weighted punching bag dolls, every time somebody pushes you over, you pop right up again. Being centered, in other words, is having a firm hold on your own sense of balance.

Now, achieving this happy state is not an over-night task; it takes time, and often a lot of hard work. But before you get discouraged about the prospect of achieving it yourself, you should know that there is one thing you can do right now to begin regaining your balance: set a goal.

I've already talked about the importance of having a goal, and I hope I've helped you see how crucial it is to balance. But seeing is not the same as doing, and you may still be wondering how to go about it. You've been down for a long time, and naturally you can't just hop up now on my say-so. You're perplexed about which goal to choose. You're afraid to select a goal which may prove to be wrong for you. You're torn between immediate, short-term goals and long-term, grand dreams.

Even though I can't tell you specifically which goal is best for you, I can tell you which *kind* of goal might be best. Generally speaking—and especially when you're depressed—it's best to start with a modest, achievable goal for the immediate future. Determine, for example, to spend a set number of hours studying a particular subject or practicing a sport or musical instrument. Leave off dreaming about moon shots for a couple of weeks; once you get your first, immediate goals met, you can gradually work up to greater things.

Then, once you set a short-term objective, keep track of your progress. Keep a notebook or just write down on scratch paper how much time you spend at your chosen task each day. Gradually try to increase the time spent, and this will build up your confidence and ability to achieve longer range goals.

If you find yourself getting bored with the task you have set, perhaps it's time to make it more challenging: make it more complex or shoot for a higher level of performance. Experience will tell you which goals are challenging but attainable for you, and you can adjust your sights and efforts accordingly. Experience, too, will show you how hard you are willing to work for something, how distractable you are and how you actually want to parcel out your time.

Now, it's very easy, when we're setting out plans for ourselves, to scatter our shots so wide that we never get anything done. We may convince ourselves that our interests are too broad to be confined by a simple design, but actually this frequently becomes a way of avoiding the effort needed to finish any one task. As the Englishman Sir Henry Bulwer noted: "The man who seeks but one thing in life may hope to achieve it; but he who seeks all things only reaps, from the hopes which he sows, a harvest of barren regrets." You may not want to limit yourself to one goal, but unless you *start* with only one, you'll never get to the ten, or ten thousand, of which you may eventually be capable.

The more specifically you can define your goal, the easier it will be for you to establish priorities and determine what you are willing to do to make your reality conform to your dreams. This sounds simplistic but it is true. Most people know what it takes to succeed in various endeavors, but are unwilling to make the sacrifices, run the risks or do what it takes to become who they want to be.

There's no magic involved in the connection between goals and contentment. Think of it this way. Having a goal will eliminate a basic frustration in your life and one of the major sources of your distress: your lack of purpose. Knowing where you are headed makes getting there that much easier.

For example, you may wish that school were over and you were already working at the job of your choice. Well, if you make that job your immediate goal, and then focus on the tasks (such as schoolwork) that you must complete in order to attain it, you'll be surprised how much more bearable hitting the books will be. Realistically you probably know that your prospects will improve once you have a diploma; even if you hate school, then, you'll get through it better if you think of it as a necessary step toward your objective.

Certain steps are essential for certain goals. If you want to go to graduate school, you'll have to finish college with good grades first. If you want to be a carpenter in Maine, you will have to learn about hammers and saws. Acquiring the requisite skills can be a real pleasure when you view it as preparation for attaining a desirable goal.

Having faith that you will reach your goal, you will be able to relax and function in a way which maximizes your assets. Rather than scatter your energy in many directions, distracted by friends' and parents' advice, you will begin to focus on that narrower range of activities which you do best.

I don't mean that you should immediately focus on a single objective, and forget about all other interests. You couldn't do that even if you tried, and in fact sometimes it's a real advantage to be able to dream beyond that immediate goal. In the short run, give it all you've got. But in the broader perspective, don't be afraid to listen to your daydreams—especially the ones that seem impossible. Time spent in daydreaming and fantasy about the future can be extremely useful, particularly if you allow yourself the luxury of considering all of your thoughts, even the ones you think are ridiculous. Your parents and friends may advise you to be more "serious" in your thinking, but it's you, not they, who know what you really want. Our society puts a great stock in rational approaches to living, but the seed of most great achievements, whether on the gridiron or in the laboratory, is an unrealized and often impractical idea or daydream. Genius, said Thomas Edison, is two percent inspiration and ninety-eight percent perspiration. You know that the sweat is important, but that doesn't mean you should forget about the other two percent.

You may be tempted to say that Edison was not typical. He was exceptional, and you are just an ordinary person. You can't be expected to achieve his kind of results, no matter how much you dream or work.

If you're thinking this, you should remember that Edison became exceptional; he wasn't born that way. And he achieved his success by following precisely the kind of advice I'm suggesting: he set himself a goal, and then worked to achieve it, ignoring the admonitions of older and wiser souls who told him it just couldn't be done.

Keep in mind, too, what I said earlier about the intrinsic value of goals. Pursuit of a meaningful objective is fundamentally of value not because of the significance of the goal itself, or because of the success you'll achieve because of it, but because it challenges you and brings out your own untapped abilities. This is why it is important to strive, because only then can you really test your limits and discover your strengths. The sooner you fix a goal for yourself, the more comfortable and ultimately satisfying your life will be, because when you set a goal, you develop a sense of mastery and control over yourself.

How much you accomplish relative to others doesn't matter. What matters is how high you strive relative to your *own* ability. Moving beyond your own base line will give you a sense of achievement and personal discovery, and it is of almost no consequence in which area of activity you choose to do that—as long as you select something which has meaning and significance for you.

All the feelings that are making you miserable—your sense of failure, lack of worth and recognition, resentment and boredom—will start to fade away once you start making a real effort to pursue meaningful goals. As you know by now, you cannot get rid of these feelings by looking on the bright side. What you need is something to galvanize your energies away from morose reflection and toward self-approval. A goal will serve this function beautifully.

You can maximize your chances of fulfilling your objectives, moreover, if you remember my earlier advice about planning. Your plans do not have to be elaborate, but the clearer you are about what you want to accomplish, the more likely will be your success.

Sit down for a half-hour each day with a pencil and paper. Write down all your thoughts about possible goals—everything you might want to accomplish or obtain or become. Try for three or four thoughts a day. Don't worry about how foolish some of them seem to be. This is for your eyes only. In a month you'll have about a hundred ideas to examine, and from these you can begin to discern a pattern of interests. Somewhere in that pattern will be one or more ideal immediate goals.

Go over your list and decide on one thing you want more than the rest. It may be a small thing—passing algebra, getting along better with your father, earning some spending money, learning to play the guitar—or it may be a major objective like becoming an astronaut, getting a good job, going to California, becoming a salmon fisherman in Alaska or getting your own apartment. Whatever it is, write your objective on a small piece of paper, carry it with you always and start thinking every day about how to achieve it.

It might help to imagine that the goal is not your own, but someone else's. Try thinking through how you would advise someone else who wanted to do the same thing. Stand back from yourself long enough to see what your advice would be to a friend aiming for your goal. Write that advice down, and step by step try to follow it. If you think about your goal every day, you will gradually find yourself overcoming the inevitable problems and obstacles along the way to achieving it.

"But what if that doesn't happen?" you say. What if this method of self-observation and daily planning just doesn't work for you?

What you're really asking is: "What if I fail again?"

Many people don't try things because they are afraid they'll be embarrassed, or look foolish, or feel inadequate, if they aren't instant successes. They refuse to run the risk of failing, forgetting that, no matter how capable they are, they are always going to run into situations which tax their resources beyond their limits, and which therefore set them up for a fall. In fact the more successful you have been in the past and the more challenging your objectives now, the more, rather than less, opportunity you will have to fail in the future. That's just the nature of striving.

Because of this, I can't give you a guarantee of success. Nobody can. But I can point out a couple of things I've learned in many years of talking to young people in exactly your situation. One is that failures offer you a chance to learn and improve what you're doing, to look for new ways to accomplish what you want. In this way, they can actually be a plus. Remember that winners are people who have failed many times but have learned from their defeats. As Wendell Phillips said, defeat is "nothing but education, nothing but the first step to something better."

The other thing I've learned from young people who have overcome depression is that you can't really fail if you shoot for a goal that means something to you. You can only fail when your objective isn't your own; following other people's goals will mean you are bound to fail even if you publicly succeed. People who succeed at other people's objectives are frequently frustrated, unhappy and at a loss to explain the emptiness of their lives.

Most people don't believe that they can become what they want to become, so they don't even try, and of course they don't make it. But if you take stock of your dreams and begin to act on them consciously, you'll soon discover that they are becoming part of your reality. In the process you will become more competent, more knowledgeable, more centered and more certain of yourself.

Remember that nobody is holding you back from your goal—not the world, your parents, your teachers or anyone else. Only *you* can hold you back, and you do this generally because of a fear of looking bad to other people. Keep in mind that looking foolish to others never lasts very long, and if you can learn to accept this kind of trivial discomfort for ten or twenty minutes at a time, it will pass and you can get on to the business at hand. Practice timing the duration of those feelings of discomfort: you'll be surprised, I think, at how quickly they disappear when, rather than worrying about them, you simply observe them and let them pass.

Now, maybe you can't do all this the first time out. That's why doing "life plan" exercises daily is important. Start each day with a set of objectives you want to accomplish that day. Maybe Monday you want to call your school about a photography course; Tuesday you want to investigate that job at the mill; Wednesday you'll give your room that overdue cleaning; and so on. Keep a diary of everything you do—what happened, how you spent your time—and at the end of the day or week or month, you will be able to see whether you are spending enough time and effort on reaching your designated goal. This will give you some feedback which you can then use to revise your planning and efforts.

If you find you can't accomplish the daily objectives you set for yourself, divide your activity into smaller units. If you can't get moving at all, try setting your sights a little lower. If you're depressed, it's absurd to expect yourself to achieve what you would normally achieve. Your objective for the day might be simply to get up and go to the grocery store, or cook yourself a steak. It could be to skim over some easy part of your homework or to tackle the simplest, most mechanical part of a job. Sometimes planning just one activity per hour can be helpful. As you feel better, you can set more challenging tasks.

So plan your day, every day. Before you go to sleep at night, or first thing in the morning, set up the day's activities so you'll know what's ahead of you. When you plan before you have to act, you'll avoid indecision and the confusion of meeting too many choices each day. This will also help you keep focused on what it is you really want to do.

As you make your schedule, you should visualize the upcoming activities in your mind. Close your eyes, relax, and see yourself doing the things you've set out to do. Focus first on activities that are easy and that cause you the least frustration. That way, you'll be able to progress to harder things as the day goes on.

When the day is over, you might want to review your progress before you go to bed. As the Roman philosopher Seneca noted, if every night we "call ourselves to account . . . our vices will abate of themselves if they are brought every day to the shrift." Going over your successes and failings each night is a way of keeping track of where you are, and what you still have to do to accomplish your goals.

And remember, you can't do everything. If you overcommit yourself, if you take on more tasks than you're comfortably able to handle, you'll get yourself buried in responsibilities for which you don't have sufficient energy. You may end up unable to do anything at all because you are feeling so pushed. You've already been pushing and overextending yourself, remember? And it hasn't worked out so well. So back off for a while. Don't be intimidated by people who want you to do them "tiny" favors that take time away from your plan. You've been intimidated long enough, and you can afford to be selfish for a while—at least until things are moving more smoothly for you.

This is your life, after all. A real friend will understand that, and will know that there are some things you simply have to do for yourself before you can begin taking on extra chores.

You must understand that too. You must learn to take care of yourself. You must be willing to go it alone in pursuit of your objectives and not worry about the approval or the abuse of others.

Naturally you're going to make mistakes. You may fail to learn from the past, or review alternate ways of approaching problems, or consider all relevant variables when making your choices. You may find yourself moving on to whatever new approach comes immediately to mind rather than planning the next strategy carefully. Any of these things can lead to failure.

But so what? Edison failed plenty. We all have. Failure is no proof of worthlessness. Seen calmly, it can be a spur to further achievement.

When you're frustrated, it's easy to become anxious, and anxiety in turn can lead to confusion, bad planning, mistakes—and more frustration. That's why it's necessary sometimes simply to slow down, to wait before making that next decision, to ignore the flurry of advice around you and consider slowly and quietly what's best for you.

You may be so uncomfortable with indecision and so impatient that you act quickly to eliminate the anxiety of uncertainty. Quick decisions, however, frequently cause you more anxiety in the end. One of the most important, and hardest, things to learn is how to *tolerate* uncertainty and delay your responses when such a delay will help you come up with a better solution. By learning to live with temporary anxiety, you can work toward eliminating the real, long-range anxiety that has been bothering you for so long.

A basic principle to keep in mind here is that each moment offers you an opportunity to test new ways of behaving. What has happened up to now is history. It need not determine what you choose to do next.

Try to recall how you usually make a decision in a crisis. You may handle crisis situations extremely well because you have no time to consider the opinions of others or the possibilities of error. When not in a crisis, you may feel obliged to discuss your personal decisions with others, and this can simply confuse the issue. You may, in seeking advice, be trying to rationalize your own indecisiveness, or creating alibis. It's always easier to blame others rather than yourself for inaction.

Sure, it's possible to reduce your anxiety by talking to others. But when you do this, you also reduce the chances of developing your own real confidence. In fact, you reinforce your dependency on others and set the stage for stress. If you become increasingly dependent on "expert" opinions, you will be reluctant to do anything on your own. The very act of seeking advice to make you feel more secure in your plans and decisions can, paradoxically, make you feel less secure. Step-by-step decisions, like the overall scope of your life, are ultimately *your* responsibility. If you do need help in getting going and want the advice of others, you would be well advised to seek the help of professionals such as your minister, school guidance counselor or family doctor, all of whom are trained in the art of helping others without being so heavy-handed as to discourage individual initiative or encourage dependency.

V

Self-observation, planning, setting goals—these are all very well, I can hear you saying, but what you don't realize is that other people make it really tough for me to concentrate on what I want. They're always getting in the way, telling me what to do. My parents, most of all. What can I do to get them off my back?

There's no doubt that you're in a tricky position with your parents. It's not at all easy being an adolescent. On the one hand, you're beginning to look and speak like an adult, and therefore are beginning to experience that wonderful feeling of having people view you independently of your family. On the other hand, your parents, who have known you since infancy, can't possibly see you the way the world does: for them, past perceptions are still vivid, and you are still a child. As long as you are living at home, this can generate tension. Naturally you want to assert yourself and dismiss your parents' advice. After all, the world relates to you as if you were an adult. Why should you have any patience with people who still think of you as a kid?

Here you are, physically an adult who can't get by with a half-price ticket on a plane, and your parents still expect you to be home at a certain time, and then to give them a full report on where you've been, what you've been doing, how much money you've spent and what friends you've seen. No wonder you feel angry and resentful. You feel as if they're spying on you, giving you the third degree and demonstrating no trust for you at all. All of this intensifies your sense of inadequacy and guilt, and you blame them for the subsequent bad feelings.

Many parents of teenagers—I'd say most of them, in fact—get on their children's nerves like this at one time or another. Why? Why do they do this to you?

Well, to understand why, you might begin by remembering that you're not the only one going through a period of rapid growth. Your parents are doing that too, and it's not exactly a snap for them. Ever since you were a baby, they've been the ones calling the shots, helping you out, telling you what to do, guiding you as well as they knew how. Now, suddenly, you're a grown-up, and you want no part of their help. Of course this upsets and confuses them.

Your parents have helped you create your self-image, your sense of self-acceptance and your view of the world. But they are not responsible for you any more, and you rightly don't expect them to be. They're not so sure about this, though. The fact that you are growing up and are about to move away soon can be very threatening to your parents, because it indicates to them that they are moving into the next stage of their lives as well. Secretly they probably wish you would stay a child forever, because that would mean they would stay young forever too. Your new independence, then, is making them feel left behind.

Until now, they assumed most of your responsibilities for you, so they're not well prepared for the change. Maybe they didn't expect it to occur so soon. Maybe they are anxious about handing over your life to you because they are afraid you're not ready to handle it. It might look like they just want to lord it over you, but keep in mind that your adolescence is awakening in them certain anxieties left over from their own adolescence. No doubt they sometimes project these anxieties onto you, but that's out of confusion, not maliciousness.

You say your parents constantly deemphasize your strengths and focus on your weaknesses. The way they view you implies that you're never going to develop the requisite skills you need to become an adult. The end result is that you are afraid to act on your own—another self-fulfilling prophecy.

This is a bad state of affairs, no doubt about it, but before you condemn them for keeping you down, let me see if I can show you some ways in which you might actually be contributing to the situation yourself.

In effect your parents have put you in the role of a scapegoat because of needs they themselves have. That's bad, but haven't you made things worse by going along with their definition of you? Haven't you learned to play the scapegoat role so as not to disappoint their unspoken need for you to remain their child? Don't you in some ways prove they are right—that you are not mature enough to decide matters for yourself? Don't you, instead of explaining how you feel, hold it all inside, feeding right into the idea that you are uncooperative or moody, like a sulking little kid?

Compliance with parental expectations and reluctance to express yourself can build up guilt and resentment in you, and the more you hold things in, the more the tension will continue to mount. This in turn may lead to an explosion, which will only aggravate your parents further, because it will be evidence that you are not only a child, but a bad one as well. Viewing the fluctuations in your mood as evidence not of confusion but of misconduct, they may seek to quiet the anxiety it causes them by punishing you.

Adolescents frequently let themselves in for this kind of misunderstanding, since they're almost as confused about their growing up as their parents are. But if you go along with the naughty child role, you're making real trouble for yourself.

Parents generally react in one of two ways to a naughty child. If they focus on your overt behavior rather than what you are feeling, they may take a moralistic view and may resort to discipline rather than considering whether or not they had any part in creating your problems. Impatient, confused and guilty, they may demand that you simply change your ways, even though that may be beyond your immediate capacity.

On the other hand, they may go overboard in the opposite direction. They may become abnormally helpful and "understanding," in a way that actually minimizes the seriousness of your problems. Influenced by their own anxieties and by the erroneous belief that adolescence is always terribly stressful, they may go out of their way not to yell at you or make demands.

But whether they use the hard-line or the soft-pedal approach, they give evidence that they are out of touch with what you are really going through.

Sometimes, this will tempt you to say, "The hell with them, I don't need them any more." You may feel that you've grown so far away from them that they couldn't influence you even if they tried. That's an understandable reaction, but if you think about it, you'll see it's not really on target. The truth is that, whether you like it or not, your parents are extremely influential in determining how you feel. Whether you view them as good or bad parents, as loving or unloving, as supportive or destructive, their influence on you is unavoidable. What you have to do is find a way to deal with it effectively.

You say you are trying to establish an independent life-style, but that this is hard to do when you're living at home and especially when you depend on your parents' financial assistance. It seems they're always looking over your shoulder.

You may be right. But try to think of *why* they may be such constant nags. Is it because they want to keep you dependent on them forever, or out of a perverse desire to make you miserable? Probably not. Most parents, though it's painful for them to confront it, actually look forward to their children's independence, because it will give them a freedom they have not experienced since they were young. But they are not going to readily relinquish control over you while they sense you're having difficulties. Maybe it seems like their help is just a string of orders. But remember that, like everybody else, parents are frequently clumsy in expressing their concern. It may seem impossible to please them, but they may feel the same way toward you. Because they are just as anxious as you to be loved, they may overreact to your slightest criticism or mistake, concluding that there's no communication at all between you.

So the tension and feelings of rejection that you talk about may well be mutual. You're probably rejecting them as often as they're rejecting you. Sure, you crave special attention in this troubling time. But so do they.

I don't doubt that your parents are less sensitive to you than you would like. But try to think why they might be acting like this. At this point in your life, they have their own serious troubles. They too are going through a crisis. Your father may be under pressure at work and may simply be letting some of his frustrations out on you. Your mother may feel uncertain about her role now that you are grown. In addition, each of them is used to dealing with you in a different way, and in these tense times that may be causing tension between them. You may be getting some of the flak from that tension. As they battle to resolve the loose ends of their relationship with you, accusing you of intransigence may seem a safer solution than actually confronting their own inadequacies.

There's no doubt about it. Your parents are inconsistent. Not only are they fumbling about in their parental roles, but they are often confusing their own experiences with yours. What can you do about it? How can you get them off your back?

You can begin by seeing them in perspective, as people with their own personalities, traits, virtues, problems, desires, interests, histories, faults and fears. Remembering that you are not responsible for any of these factors will make it easier for you to be objective about them.

Next, you can start being very careful about how you react to them when they annoy you. Anger, said Clarendon, is "the most impotent of passions. If effects nothing it goes about, and hurts the one who is possessed by it more than the one against whom it is directed." Lashing out at somebody who seems to be nagging or berating you, I know, often seems like the only reasonable response. All it is, however, is the quickest response; very seldom is it the best. So the first rule to remember when a fight is in the air is to disengage from the fray. Wait a moment before speaking. Listen to what they are saying. Don't give advice unless you're asked for it.

And don't *solicit* advice either. A common trap in parent-child arguments is for the child to ask the parents for an opinion, then get angry when the opinion is not what the child wanted to hear. Once you have asked for guidance, you will only cause conflict if you act contrary to the way you have been advised. Acting first and discussing the matter afterwards, therefore, can often be a far better choice than asking for advice, acting as if you plan to follow it, and then doing just the opposite to demonstrate your "independence." This is pseudoindependence, and a way of rejecting responsibility. This kind of behavior suggests that you are pushing your parents to the limit to find out if they really care about you enough to tell you to stop. Many of us test our superiors this way, and it very seldom has a good effect.

I am not advocating passivity. I'm just suggesting that confrontations generally make matters worse. Argument breeds argument and leads to rules, restrictions and new demands—especially if your parents are worried about you. Don't feed their anxiety by doing and saying things you know very well will only set them off.

For example, if your father objects to your smoking in the house, don't argue with him that you're old enough to smoke if you want to. Simply don't smoke in front of him. Do it someplace else. Since your mother gets upset when you come home late, get into the habit of calling her late in the evening to reassure her you're all right. Don't purposely avoid doing something that's important to them; that will only provoke them, and waste your energy in avoidable power struggles.

You may be letting your parents take responsibility for areas of your life that are really yours to control. You may, having involved them in your decision-making, express surprise that they fail to treat you as an independent adult. Since dependency can be disguised in many ways, you may be asking them for advice without even realizing it. When you tell them all your plans, for example, you invite their approval or disapproval. In effect this is like asking for permission. If your parents disapprove of your plans, whether you grudgingly cooperate or angrily rebel, you have already included them in your decision. Recognizing this, you should be able to take responsibility for your requests; the best course may be to abide by the judgment you have invited, and the next time keep your plans to yourself.

Here's an example. Say you have saved some money from a summer job and want to invest in guitar lessons. You are enthusiastic about the guitar but your parents' musical taste and general attitude differ from yours. You know that if you ask their advice, they'll tell you to save your money or go back to piano lessons. Since that would go against your own desires, wouldn't it make sense, in this kind of a situation, simply to make the decision yourself, without consulting them? If you act on your own, thereby assuming responsibility for yourself, your parents will not have to feel obliged to tell you what's "best" for you. You will have made a free choice—good or bad—for yourself, and your parents will have to respect you for it.

Of course, not all your choices will be good ones. But not all your parents' choices are good either, and it's far better to act on your own bad choice than on somebody else's possibly good one. Putting pressure on your parents by asking them to decide for you is a way of maintaining the very dependency you say you resent. Learn to decide as much as possible for yourself, and in time you will know when it is best to rely on the judgment of others and when you can rely on your own. Until you stop constantly testing the waters for approval, however, you will not learn to take responsibility for yourself.

Learning to keep your own counsel, to trust your instincts, and to act accordingly, is never easy. But this is your life, after all. Ultimately you are going to be on your own, and the sooner you can learn to make your own decisions, the sooner your parents will accept the fact that you can in fact manage without them. When you complain that you're not getting their permission to do what you want, you're saying that you feel like a disgruntled child. If that's how you present yourself to them, that's how they're going to treat you.

You don't have to be sassy or contentious to let your parents know you're capable of making your own decisions. When your mother asks, "When are you coming home?" just answer the question. You don't have to give an exact time, just a reassuring estimate. "I don't know for sure," you might say, "but it won't be too late." If your father asks where you are off to, recognize that the question reflects his concern for you, not a need to control you. If you consider your parents' concerns, in other words, you won't feel compelled to respond sharply or defensively. A simple answer sometimes will work wonders.

It's hard enough for you to figure out what you want. Why complicate the issue by adding in the expectations and demands of your parents? Even if they're similar to your own, once you learn to follow your own advice first, both you and your parents will be relieved. Believe me, they don't like breathing down your neck any more than you like it, but at the moment they feel they've got to control your life, because you're not doing it yourself. As your behavior changes, their anxiety will diminish and they'll learn to stop acting on your behalf.

If you aren't accustomed to choosing for yourself, the realization that you're the one in charge of your life can be overwhelming. When you take charge of yourself, you automatically give up that nice warm feeling of support you had when you were sure your parents would take care of you and come up with all the right answers. This can make you feel lonely and anxious, and sometimes it can even aggravate family tensions. But that's temporary. Learning to ride out the discomfort and anxiety of acting on your own, without parental approval, is one of the tensely exciting tasks of adolescence. "The best government," the German writer Goethe observed, is "that which teaches us to govern ourselves." The more you can learn to rely on yourself, ultimately the less complicated your life will be.

So don't be afraid to keep some things to yourself. Sure, honesty is essentially a great policy, but that doesn't mean that you have to see your parents as confessors, rightfully privy to your every whim and fancy. When you are open about everything, you invite criticism and pressure. Learn to parcel out your confessions judiciously. Complaining every time you feel down will just send your parents up the wall, because it will make them feel guilty and responsible. Remember that your feelings, no less than your behavior, are your responsibility too.

Now, I can't guarantee that, if you practice the kind of understanding, judicious silence and self-reliance I've been talking about, you'll never have another flare-up with your folks. No matter how cautious you are, occasionally you're still bound to feel put upon, and that feeling is going to push you to the breaking point.

When that happens, I'd ask you to try out a technique I've found very useful for defusing antagonism. It's simply to *delay your responses*. You don't have to delay them for long; a few minutes will do. But fight the urge to blow up the moment you first see red. The most common automatic reaction to pressure—a display of anger—can often cause more problems than the pressure itself. Remember that you don't have to defend yourself or make decisions under fire. When your parents criticize you or make demands, don't react immediately; if you're pressed for an answer, tell them you'll let them know as soon as you can. Wait until things cool down and then decide.

Confrontations are rarely of value. They frighten you and your parents, and you may all become more demanding because each of you fears losing control of the situation. Even if you do gain a point by fighting, you may feel uneasy about your victory because it came as the result of an unfriendly conflict.

Delaying your responses, I realize, may go very much against the grain of your normal family interactions. Especially in families, people generally relate to each other in fixed patterns, with each person playing an expected role; conflict is often built into the normal patterns. You'll be amazed, though, once you become aware of your own fixed-role patterns, how you can change them simply by taking some time out and refusing to act automatically, like a robot.

Think back to what I said about taking notes instead of reacting peevishly to that verbose friend on the telephone. You can use a similar technique in direct, face-to-face communication. Take mental notes. Review for yourself what is said and what is decided. Ask your parents to do the same, and compare notes with them. Problems frequently come up when two people, usually a parent and a child, forget what they said and have different versions of a single conversation. You can avoid this problem by consciously comparing versions.

This means, of course, that your parents and you must learn to listen to each other. You can resolve a lot of problems if you can discuss the issues instead of adopting a defensive posture and yelling. Sometimes you need their feedback, so ask for their thoughts and give them a chance to analyze what's going on. This is not the same thing as asking for advice. It's just a way of getting all the information you can about the situation before deciding what you think about it.

Some of the information they give you may not be pleasant to hear, but you should welcome it anyway. Sometimes criticism given in a calm, deliberate attempt to clarify a situation can be more useful than praise. Observations about your shortcomings, as Quarles noted, can be either just or unjust, but either way they are useful: "Make use of both," he counsels, "so shall thou distil honey out of gall, and out of an open enemy make a secret friend."

By asking thoughtful questions, paying attention to the answers, quelling your anger, and attempting to understand, you will make relations with your parents much easier than they have been up to now. Once they see you are taking them seriously and not just trying to buck them, they won't have to come on so strong. If you talk quietly and sincerely, without belligerence, you'll see a difference in their response. Parents, too, want to be treated as individuals with importance and dignity, and tricky as it sometimes is, you can learn to do this without surrendering control of your life.

VI

What I've been saying applies not only to your relationships with your parents, but to other relationships as well. Your parents are probably the worst offenders against your sense of personal integrity, but if you let them, your friends and even your casual acquaintances can also get in your way far more than is healthy for any of you. Among human beings, there is never a shortage of people who would prefer to run other people's lives rather than their own, and they'll readily make things tough for you even while they seem to be offering help.

But—and it's an important but—they'll do this only if you let them. If other people, as you say, are imposing on you, that's very probably because you subtly invite them to do so. You know that your behavior influences the behavior of others toward you, so if you are constantly getting into arguments, for example, you might do well to find out if you are setting yourself up for them.

Do you do anything that makes people feel free to impose on you? Do you smile and look agreeable when someone asks you for a favor—and then grumble in private? Is there something in your attitude or manner that leads other people to reject or annoy you? Do you check everything out with others before you act? Do you tell others everything you do so they can tell you what they think of it?

What I am suggesting is that you may be creating your own stress, even in situations where others seem to be the cause of it. It's always easier to blame others, but as the medieval monk Saint Bernard pointed out, "Nothing can work me damage except myself. The harm that I sustain I carry about me, and never am a real sufferer but by my own fault."

I'll give you a specific example. Suppose you're living with a roommate who is a goof-off, and you feel you'd be under less pressure if only he would do more of the household chores and not leave you with all the work. Everything would be fine, you think, if he were more cooperative.

Having him cooperate more sounds like a good idea, but do you act as if you think that's a real option? Or do you do his work for him, complaining all the while? If you're taking up all the slack, there's no real reason for him to work harder. If you cover for him like this, you're operating not as an individual, but as part of a self-perpetuating system which sustains both his indolence and your resentment.

A wise approach, in this kind of situation, might be not to tell your friend off, but simply to let certain chores go by the boards. Maybe, if you let certain things go undone, he would see the need of his increased cooperation. You would be running the risk, of course, that things would not work out to your satisfaction, but at least you wouldn't continue to feel responsible and resentful. And it couldn't make matters much worse, could it?

The point I'm making is that you never do yourself any good by taking on other people's tasks grudgingly. If you like the extra work, fine. If not, you're only putting yourself in a martyr role, probably to cover up feelings of personal inadequacy. This can only undercut you, because martyrdom feeds all too readily into the familiar pattern of resentment, repression of feelings, guilt and more resentment. We've already seen what a mess that can get you into.

I'm aware, of course, that to some extent Society does contribute to your dissatisfaction and stress. As long as you live with other people, there will be some conflict between how you behave and how others feel you should behave. No matter how hard you try, you're bound to keep running into people who will try to pressure you into behaving their way rather than your own. That will lead to conflict, misunderstanding, even broken friendships and separations.

Since you say that your first close relationship has recently ended, I know you're no stranger to the poignancy and pain of separation. Maybe I should talk a little bit about the specific problems of romantic relationships, so you'll know that your situation, painful as it is, is not unique.

All the difficulties of communicating with other people are aggravated in romantic alliances. For you as an adolescent, these difficulties can seem overpowering, because nothing has prepared you for them. Your confusion about relating to other people in general is bad enough; when you compound that with all the bewildering little twitches of sexual attraction, the result can be devastating. Although, ironically, your experiences now with love and separation will prepare you for later, adult experiences, I know they can often seem like nothing so much as a bad, unending dream.

Teenage love can be awfully confusing, because our standards of conduct and norms of behavior are not only mixed, but rapidly changing. I can understand how difficult it must be for you, given your eagerness to find yourself, your fear of being exploited, your uncertainty of acceptance and your hunger for affection. No wonder you're in a cloud about the differences between love and sex, between love and friendship, and between the way you think and the way the other sex seems to think. Sometimes it seems as if you and "they" have been raised in two entirely different cultures.

The important thing to remember here is that relationships, sexual or otherwise, generally work best where both parties have a common objective and a common outlook on life. "Falling in love" is never enough; the relationships which last are formed by people who share things. That, I'm afraid, is part of the reason that so many teenage marriages fail: they're made not in heaven, as the partners seem to think, but here on earth between people who are still uncertain of what they really want out of life. All too often they discover, after the honeymoon, that they have nothing in common but a rapidly fading idea about "being in love." At the first real conflict, they find out to their chagrin that the hearts-and-flowers folks were just full of it: love does *not* conquer all.

Romantic strife is inevitable simply because it's hard, in the best of circumstances, for human beings to accept each other—accept their differences, I mean, as well as their likenesses. Once you discover your soul mate has a blemish, the temptation is to wipe it out and make him or her over into the perfect partner once again. Naturally this causes trouble, because few people want to be made over into another's image, no matter how much they like you.

It takes a while to learn not to try to change others over into your conception of how they ought to be. To some extent you may become bossy and demanding to counterbalance your inclination to go along, resentfully, with demands that rub you the wrong way. Conversely, when you make demands and others fail to respond satisfactorily, you also feel resentment. This pattern of alternating bossiness and submissiveness reflects an excessively dependent and unstable relationship which is likely to end abruptly, leaving everyone feeling devastated.

Since you've just been devastated in this way, you are probably ambivalent about whether to try to establish a close relationship with anyone else again. Because of your natural fear of rejection, you're wary of taking the initiative, and at the same time annoyed by those who approach you. What can you do about this?

Well, it may seem paradoxical, but the first principle to follow in building up your capacity to relate to others is that old standby, self-reliance. Especially after a breakup. A breakup sometimes can be a blessing in disguise, in that it impels you to reexamine your own life, to demand of yourself that you begin to take care of your own needs, since no one else (apparently) is willing to do it for you. Only when you can do that will you be able to love freely, without the burden of needing someone to tell you you're OK.

For most young people, relationships with the opposite sex, very difficult to establish under the best of conditions, are frequently aggravated by an abundance of confusing sex drives. This is a knotty problem for adolescents—and for the rest of humanity as well—so I know what you mean when you say that you very often feel "all mixed up" about it. One year ago you couldn't care less about the opposite sex. Now, all of a sudden, you are having a big effect on them, and they on you—and you don't quite know what to do about it.

You're distressed about the power that some people now seem to possess over you. No doubt this accounts for the impact of the rejection you experienced when your friend suggested you both start seeing other people. To judge from your letter, you haven't got over that yet.

I have no sugar pills to help you get over that hurt, and I'm certainly not going to minimize its intensity. But it might help you to know that, even thought it's ended, your experience with a thwarted love might well prove to be illuminating and helpful to you in the future. Corny as it sounds, it *is* better to have loved and lost than never to have loved at all—not because it's morally right but because it widens the scope of your sensitivity, your ability to continue to grow.

I'm not trying to make you feel better, just stating a condition. The excitement and beauty of a first love has probably triggered tremendously positive forces in you, among them the capacity to be open and vulnerable to others. Your experience has made you willing for one of the few times in your life to share that life with another person. That's no mean gift. It's so powerful, in fact, that when thwarted it can easily turn into rancor, or envy or regret.

Yet what links those emotions is an unrealistic attraction to lost causes. You can *profit* from your broken heart, but only if you first feel, and then go beyond, the pain.

You know now that it's only from others that you can discover certain hidden facets of your own character and personality; it's only in loving contact with other people that you enrich and broaden yourself. At the same time, though, the experience has left you feeling wasted and used up. This is an unpleasant paradox of love.

Yet you are willing to talk about your feelings. This is really terrific, believe me—even if you still feel vulnerable. For if you closed yourself off to protect yourself entirely, you might have felt relieved temporarily, but in the end you would have stopped growing as a person, and that wouldn't have made you feel good at all. You would have become like the anodyned, terrified character in the song, "I am a rock, I am an island," ostensibly content "because a rock feels no pain, and an island never cries." It's really a plus, therefore, to still be feeling the pain.

There are certain problems involved, though. When you let your defenses down and you let others tune into your real feelings about yourself (and them), you feel so close to them that your sense of self begins to merge, to mesh, with their responses to you and your feelings toward them. You create a "third person" that is the composite of you both, and this third person, like the two of you, gets thrown into a big emotional stew, in which you often feel so absorbed that you don't see how you ever functioned alone. When this intense sense of closeness and dependency comes to an end, it can make you feel like the world has also stopped. That's the unhappy paradox: if you hadn't opened yourself up so much, you wouldn't be feeling so rotten right now.

You may truly believe that you won't be able to continue living without your friend. You may be able to say, with Skeeter Davis, that it's the end of the world. But when you think about it soberly, you know that's a notion based on a false appraisal of the world. You can go on living without him or her, and you will, in spite of any songs. Which is why you really should be envied, not pitied. You've just learned one of the greatest lessons of your life. You should be grateful enough for that to take a good look at it and see how it can help you in the future.

Love and separation are experiences you must go through in order to develop the capacity to have close relationships with others, and there is no way to to do this except in the manner in which you have done it. If you avoid such experiences in order not to be hurt, you will fail to develop the capacity to have such experiences, and that will severely limit your potential richness as a person. The more experiences you have of loving, the better you will behave in the future. Sadly, there is no way of developing this capacity without risk. But no great lesson is cheap.

You say you felt very much "alive" when you were in love. I can understand this, but wasn't there also a large amount of wishful thinking, a dependency on your relationship, as well as a belief that, if you only let things alone, they would work out by themselves? Maybe you took drowsy infatuation for awakeness, and you've only now woken up from the dream.

It it difficult to learn that love flourishes most when you are least dependent on it, and withers when you desperately need it. People who can't live without each other generally are involved in very limited, and eventually self-destructive, relationships. For love to grow and evolve, you have to be able to get along without it. This is another crucial paradox.

Why, you ask, do relationships hurt so much?

Partly because of the false assumption that you need the other person, partly because of ego, partly because openness followed by separation—even amicable separation—is experienced as rejection. Separation reactivates all our old feelings of guilt and unworthiness and self-blame. No wonder breaking up makes us feel lousy.

I know how you feel when you write about your continuing sense of loss, about your lack of being cared for by someone to whom you want to be close. No wonder you don't feel like you fit in anywhere. If a lover or just a friend rejects you, it's hard to have confidence that anyone else will accept you. But have you really examined what *you* might be doing to keep things on this unsteady ground? Remember the old monk's observation, "Nothing can work me damage except myself," and think about how you relate to others rather than how they relate to you. I can't read your mind, but maybe what's wrong with your relationships is that you pretend to share with others when in fact you are keeping your real feelings to yourself. You say you feel "bottled up." Maybe it's your hand on the cork. Maybe you're trying to protect yourself from people simply because they might hurt you as you were hurt in the past. Maybe you are reacting to others as if they're only symbolic recapitulations of something in your past. The repetition of past patterns and the constraints of habits and predetermined "life scripts" may all be contributing to your problems.

Maybe, in other words, you've been trying to fit into molds that are familiar to you—uncomfortable, perhaps, but known. Maybe part of the reason you feel blocked off from others is that they don't feel like reliving your life for you: they've got their own pasts—and presents—to contend with. They have no patience with someone who is by turns friendly and sulky, compliant and bossy, superficially open and guardedly closed.

If you try to accept the people around you as different from you, without trying to manipulate or change them, you may have better luck. At the same time, of course, you should make every effort not to allow them to control you either. The key is to improve your communications by being more honest about your feelings—this means the bad ones as well as the good ones—and the ways in which you communicate.

We're all part of a vast communications network, a system in which you trigger responses in others which in turn trigger responses in you, and so on. In effect you, unwittingly perhaps, instruct others as to how you want them to interpret what you say to them. Because this is so, you must be sensitive to the tone of your own voice, and to your attitudes, not just to the actual syllables you utter.

The development of your relationships with others is a delicate process, and I have the feeling that you have not yet begun to observe how delicate it is. Nor how malleable. That is to say, you have not yet really considered the possibility of applying rational thought to your relationships in order to adjust and improve them. I realize this goes against the common notion that love is irrational, but you can actually learn quite a bit about yourself by coolly observing your typical interactions with others. You can also learn to control the way you present yourself, by modifying not only your actual words, but your style of saying them.

Remember what I said about taking notes on your conversations? Those notes need not be limited to verbatim accounts of who spoke what to whom and when. They can include facial expressions, tones of voice and your own feelings at the time of the interaction. All of this can be very useful when you sit down to analyze your own personal style of communication.

If, for example, you note that you said, "I'll be happy to loan you five dollars" to a friend, you have a record of only one level of discourse. If, however, you also note that, while you were saying that, you thought, "This son of a bitch hasn't paid back the two I lent him last week," then you have some insight into a deeper level of significance. In this particular instance, you know that you've held an angry response in check for fear of embarrassing yourself or your friend. That would be useful to remember the next time a similar situation arose.

This brings us back, of course, to a point I've already emphasized: that you can cause yourself enormous trouble by constantly suppressing your feelings. The containment of feelings more than anything else creates feelings of anger and resentment. Doing things you don't want to do in order to please others is bound to make you resentful, and covering up the anger that's generated by such compliance only intensifies the resentment and sets into motion the old cycle of repression, guilt and more resentment.

Learn to examine your feelings. It will give you greater strength. Although feelings of fear, anger and loneliness are terribly unpleasant, you should allow yourself to experience them in order to learn to neutralize them. The greater your awareness of what you are feeling, the greater your control.

The more organized and disciplined you are about this the better. That's why I'd suggest you make a list of the ways in which you are frustrated by demands imposed on you by others, and by your own inclinations to go along with this bad script. Let the list be the answers to two questions: "What am I doing that I really don't want to be doing? What would I like to do and what's keeping me from it?" Study the list periodically, and start getting rid of the entries.

Of course, it's not easy to classify everything you do in terms of what you want to do and what you don't. Sometimes your feelings will be mixed. You may love your grandmother very much yet not want to visit her on Sunday. You may enjoy math but find you can't stand the math teacher. There will always be situations beyond your control. But you can learn to tolerate them if you try. At least by recognizing how you are feeling about the situation, and why, you may be able to ride it out. Not fight it out. Just let it flow around you, until it passes.

You can also learn to avoid those specific situations which get to you most. You can learn to keep the world off your back, and to reduce the pressures around you. When you recognize the traps, you can start bypassing them, and start living in a more selfish way.

I don't mean that negatively. What I'm talking about is not really selfishness, but self-directedness. You don't owe your friends a shot at solving problems which you can solve much better yourself. The faster you cut down on soliciting their advice the quicker you'll cut down the confusion and bad feelings which often come with such solicitation.

It's probably not advisable to discuss your recent breakup with "interested" or "concerned" friends. Not that they don't feel for you, because they probably do, but they may be too close to you to advise you sensibly, and it's certain also that their interpretations will be colored by their own histories—which may not relate very well to yours. You do not have to tell visitors or curiosity-seekers about your experiences. No matter how loudly you hear it proclaimed that you should share your insights, you should share what you want, and nothing further.

How can you tell whether to talk to a specific friend? Simple. Just consider whether you feel good, bad or worse after discussing personal matters with him or her than before. When you feel enriched by communicating with someone, go ahead. When you feel threatened or bossed around, it's probably better not to talk.

What I'm suggesting is not simple. Essentially I'm saying that you have to walk a tightrope. You must learn to behave openly and honestly without being so blunt that you invite hostility from those around you. You must learn to be open without being cruel. At the same time you must learn that you don't have to explain anything, if you don't want to, to anybody.

In other words, keep your own counsel. While being open with your feelings, don't feel obliged to confess or reveal all your deepest secrets.

That doesn't mean you should sink deeper into the shell. On the contrary it means you should keep trying all the harder to reach out to people, but doing so in a way that is not seen as threatening or abrasive. To treat them, in other words, the way you probably would like to be treated yourself: with both honesty and kindness.

VII

If you want to cut down on stress, you have to concentrate on what *you* do to bring that stress about. It may be unpleasant for you to hear that the problem is chiefly in your hands, but if you look at it objectively, that's a reassuring rather than discouraging notion. If you've essentially caused your own grief, then you can also get rid of it by yourself. There are no unseen, mysterious outside forces conspiring to keep you unhappy. There are no evil or misguided persons out to do you in. By recognizing that you're doing it all to yourself, you can begin to change it.

What I hope this letter helps you realize is that, in a host of subtle ways, you have been complicating your own life a lot more than other people or circumstances have. In dozens of ways you have been putting yourself into no-win situations. You can use your own untapped psychological resources to increase your sense of satisfaction and eliminate the things that have been making you miserable. Since your world is a reflection of your innermost thoughts, you can change the impact of external events on you simply by changing the way you view them.

The stressfulness of any situation ultimately depends on your attitude toward it. If you learn to control your emotional reactions, you will begin to see all kinds of previously overpowering situations as challenges, not obstacles. By overcoming old attitudes that color your responses and prevent you from assessing each crisis as it arises, you can learn to see nonstressful, and even exhilarating, features in every situation. By controlling your thoughts, you can condition yourself to deal with stress more effectively—to experience it, redefine it, master your responses to it, learn from it and grow.

I know that you've frequently felt rejected, felt that people just didn't understand you, or didn't want to try. That's a valid feeling, considering the things you've been going through. But what I'd like you to do is go one step further, and ask yourself whether you set yourself up to feel this way. Maybe you've been anticipating rejection by walking around with a chip on your shoulder, thus inviting people to respond to you negatively. Maybe you've been misperceiving the intentions of others by taking their statements literally instead of listening to the *way* they communicate with you. A friend, thinking of you as a strong and confident person, may make a joke at your expense without realizing how it upsets you—but if you don't let him know how you feel about it, you can't very well lay all the blame for your bad feelings at his door. People will treat you as you indicate you want to be treated; if you present yourself as someone who doesn't mind being insulted, that's exactly what you'll get.

You can't count on others to read your mind. You may think of yourself as shy, but you shouldn't be surprised if some people interpret your withdrawn attitude as evidence of snobbishness. Remember that rejection works two ways, and people may be just as afraid to approach you as you are to approach them. If you perceive this as rejection rather than evidence of their sensitivity, none of you will ever get very far in communicating.

It's natural for you to be withdrawn and skeptical now, but skepticism can cause you to overintellectualize and make incorrect assumptions about people's attitudes. That's why periodically you should examine your own behavior, and ask yourself what others see when they look at you. If you are so sensitive that you see threats to your self-esteem everywhere, you may be accusing others of a malevolence they don't possess. This is bound to frighten many people away. And it's something you can avoid by learning to examine things a little more objectively.

Dealing with other people is sometimes tricky. You have to be aware of what effect your behavior has on them, without being so influenced by their reactions that you forget who you yourself are. It's difficult to manage—so difficult in fact that all of us sometimes like to retire to the safety of our own rooms and retreat from the confusion of interpersonal relations.

This is not necessarily bad. Sometimes taking a breather from other people is just what you need. In fact it sounds to me as if you, like many of us, need to develop not only your capacity for communication, but your capacity for being alone. Sometimes being by yourself is the only thing that can increase your self-confidence and reduce your need for structured or escapist situations that keep you from becoming yourself.

The earlier in life you can get some experience in handling solitude, the more satisfactorily things will go for you later on. Solitude gives you perspective, the capacity to make your own judgments and the confidence that you can pursue your own objectives without the fear of ridicule.

When parents or friends pressure you to respond to their demands or to explain yourself, solitude is often the best way to tap into your own feelings. Remembering how you felt when last alone can also help you get a handle on your emotions, and eventually to reduce your nervous reactions to pressure.

It takes a certain amount of experience and practice to learn to be comfortable with solitude; without practice, those feelings of aloneness can easily turn into feelings of loneliness, which is not at all the same. Most of us grow up with people constantly around us, and with a strong cultural bias that being with others is desirable and being alone is bad. That's why loneliness and aloneness are often confused: it's hard to discover many of your own talents when so many books, TV shows and friends are telling you that you need others to find out who you are. Thoreau said he "never found the companion that was so companionable as solitude," but that's very easy to forget.

Yet the more you learn to rely on yourself, the more satisfactory things will be for you. This is especially true, paradoxically, when it comes to relating to other people. The person who desperately needs external evidence of his worth is much less likely to get along well with others than the person who trusts his own intuitions and designs. Solitude can enhance self-confidence, and it's self-confident people who relate best to others. So you may have to limit the time you spend in personal relationships in order to pursue your relationship with yourself more fully. You should strive to find those activities that give you the best sense of yourself, that enable you to feel good about being who you are. This takes considerable effort, but in the long run it's worth it, because it can help you reduce the tension you feel for failing to live up to the demands of others.

What I'm talking about, I guess, is a form of consciousness-raising. Until now, most of what has happened to you has happened without too much awareness or deliberation on your part. Your life has been swirling about you, tossing you this way and that like a wood chip in eddying surf. But it need not remain that way. You have the power to control your own mental processes, and the more aware you become of these processes, the greater your chance of gaining control over your life. To the extent that you can modify your thinking, you can influence what happens to you. Maybe this sounds mystical, but it's really just common sense.

"Mind over matter" is not just a guru's game; it's accessible to every one of us, every day.

Now, I know it's difficult just to snap into a new mode of thought. Patterns set in childhood have a way of holding on to you tenaciously, and some of these patterns can put a terrible crimp in your style. They can interfere with your starting to make decisions necessary to taking control of your life. Decision-making patterns tend to be based on personality and history rather than reason, and often lead you to repeat past solutions, even if they haven't worked for you before. If, for example, you follow the lead of others in searching for the best course of action, you'll continue to have trouble developing decision-making skills.

But why would you want to follow other people's leads to begin with? Don't you do that simply because you're afraid your own lead will be wrong? Isn't it your unrealistically low opinion of yourself that makes you reluctant to risk failure, and at the same time fail to see what possibilities are really available to you? And isn't this something you can change?

You have to learn to be more straightforward in making your own decisions and not worry so much about what others will think. This means that you have to develop the ability to choose wrongly and go on. Right now, because of your strong desire to please others, you sometimes accept their views against your own better judgment, and then wonder why you still get blamed for the ensuing mistakes. You can't quite understand why people are so angry with you. Think, though, of how you would feel if they constantly asked you for advice, then grumbled when it turned out wrongheaded. You'd feel resentful and guilty, and that's probably just the way others feel when you try to lay the responsibilities for your decisions on them.

It's evident that you have an inclination to be overcautious, and that this leads you to examine every alternative and weigh every consequence before making a decision. This contributes to your inability to act. Because you are so afraid of being wrong, you unnecessarily turn everyday situations into paralyzing moral and ethical dilemmas. Sometimes this leads you to act impulsively, even explosively, in order to get over the discomfort of indecision as fast as possible. In effect you are so caught up in the small issues involved in decision-making that you lose sight of your major objectives. Maybe you can understand, then, why people so often seem exasperated with you. They're simply tired of waiting for you to make up your mind, and annoyed that you seem to view every little thing in your life as a matter of life and death.

So we've got another vicious circle. Afraid of being wrong, you decide not to decide until the last minute. At that point you make a hasty choice, which proves as wrong as you feared it would in the first place. No wonder you mention panic, confused thinking and clouded memory. These are typical reactions to your problems with decision-making. You examine the same point over and over, like a needle stuck in a groove. Even your past experience cannot guide you, because your panic cuts off access to your memory. You're in another no-win situation.

But you can get out of it.

There are several mental exercises which we use in Life Strategy Workshops to get blocked young people like you moving again toward making their own decisions. Maybe some of these exercises will help you.

The first one is simply to experiment with the word "no." Try saying no to someone to whom you typically respond with a yes, or try cancelling an appointment or postponing a meeting. Try refusing some food at the table. Try not lending your notes to the friend who regularly borrows them.

More than likely, one or more of these actions will make you feel uncomfortable, because you're not used to consciously doing something you know will make others uneasy with you. (You prefer to do that unconsciously.) Persist in the exercise anyway. See how it makes you feel. Observe yourself getting upset. Bring your bad feelings to the surface, and confront them. You'll be surprised how much easier it is to feel bad when you are making a conscious effort to do so. That's a first step in mastering the negative emotion that so far has been mastering you.

As a second step, let's see if we can get rid of these bad emotions. We can do that by using a second exercise, often called the "empty jar."

The exercise may seem silly at first, but it works. In a relaxed state of mind, with eyes closed, seated in a soft chair, take three deep breaths. Let them out slowly and simply visualize an empty, uncapped jar. Then visualize yourself placing into the jar all your negative thoughts, attitudes and expectations. Put them in one by one, observing and feeling each one as you do. Put in all your unrealistic expectations of affection, love, respect and gratitude—the responses which you've been seeking, but not getting, from others. Then seal the jar and focus on a pleasant and relaxing scene.

Finally, imagine yourself putting the jar aside somewhere—on a high shelf, perhaps, or in the trash can. Once you've put it aside, you'll have a chance to discover how mistaken you were in thinking that you needed approval and support from others in the first place. You'll find that you don't need others constantly telling you you're all right in order to feel that way. You'll learn that you don't need to feel disappointed, inadequate and rejected every time your expectations don't come through. Putting aside a symbolic container of self-destructive thoughts can act to trigger insight into your own real perceptions about yourself. If you practice this technique every day—especially when you're feeling put upon by others—you'll soon find that your thoughts of rejection are just that: thoughts. As thoughts, they can be dismissed, modified, controlled.

A visualization exercise like this is useful for more than getting rid of negative feelings. It can also help you prepare yourself for positive ones— and for concrete successes. Remember what I said earlier about mentally picturing the events of each coming day in advance? Visualization techniques help psyche you up for individual decisions and events. By preparing in advance, you'll greatly enhance your chances of success in actual encounters.

The English poet Robert Southey once told an amusing anecdote about a man who always put on special glasses when he was about to eat cherries, so that "they might look bigger and more tempting. In like manner," he said, "I make the most of my enjoyments, and though I do not cast my cares away, I pack them in as little compass as I can, and carry them as conveniently as I can for myself and never let them annoy others." The visualization exercises I've been describing are like Southey's friend's glasses. They can help make your pleasures more pleasurable, your achievements more likely. At the same time, using the "empty jar" technique can help you put your worries in "as little compass" as possible—and so make even more room for your successes.

The point is to learn to control your inner turmoil rather than having it control you. If you mentally allow yourself to experience specific feelings in relation to events and circumstances, you can move progressively through the stages of observation, analysis and control. You can experience fear, self-doubt, competitiveness, acceptance and joy—without being taken over by any one of them.

When you can visualize the succession of events associated with a particular set of activities, particularly those which appear frightening, you will be amazed at the abilities you are able to uncover and the extent of what you can accomplish.

Time and again in my work with Olympic athletes I have seen this demonstrated. By visualizing the perfect stroke, the perfect swing or the perfect jump many times in the mind's eye, an athlete dramatically increases the chance of actually performing it when he begins to play. The more you can visualize the steps you will take in any activity, whether it is an athletic event, a job interview or an exam, the better prepared you will be when the situation actually arises.

Visualization exercises can actually increase your skill in performing certain tasks, reduce your anxiety and tension (and thus your chances for error), and enhance your capacity to concentrate on critical issues. They are no less useful to you than to any Olympic athlete. I have seen the techniques work with countless young people who were just as depressed as you. By visualizing things which were only dreams when they first began to think about them, the dreams came to seem real, and they were able to bring them about. By thinking through a project and focusing on the particular activities necessary to accomplish it, you endow yourself with energy and are able to accomplish far more than you ever imagined you could. We don't know precisely why this occurs, but it does.

Of course it takes some effort. Like most people, you probably cop out about eighty-five percent of the time. You're afraid to commit yourself fully to what you want—because you think the inevitable failures won't look so bad if you give the task only half a try. Because you're not comfortable going after what you want with all your energy, you approach your goals indirectly and spend time trying to get others to approve of you. You can change this, but first you must ask yourself how much time and energy you are willing to invest in what you're setting out to do. Are you focusing on the main objective or are you preoccupied with unresolved conflicts from the past? The process of growth is complex. You must be careful not to spend so much time justifying what you did in the past that you ignore new situations which can develop your talents and capacities.

Like most people, you'd like to deny responsibility for what happens to you. You complain about being constrained by your teachers and parents. You feel frustrated by many demands of convention, social pressure and divided loyalties. But up to now you've made no effort to change or modify your own responses to these demands so as to make things better for yourself. Doing that, as I hope you're beginning to see, is an essential initial step toward self-control—and contentment.

I know it's difficult to accept the view that you are the one creating the stress in your life. But this is your life, and you are responsible for what you do, the circumstances you create and what you get (or don't get) out of each day. You play a critical role—indeed, the most critical role—in the events that occur to you. Recognizing that is a start toward shaping them to your advantage.

Please don't think I'm blaming you, or trying to make you feel guilty, for what has happened to you up to now. I know it's tough to face these truths without help, and as happened to me, perhaps no one has ever told you about helicopters. Understanding that things can be different, however, is the first step toward changing them. I hope the techniques I've outlined here will give you a push, and that you'll remind yourself every day of the central point I've been trying to make: it isn't them, it's you. *You can change it all.*

VIII

This letter has been longer than I thought it would be. Let me try to tie up what I have been saying.

Your life hasn't been working for you as well as you would like, and you don't know how to get it back on the track. While it may hurt to acknowledge it, your biggest problem has been that you are not in charge.

This central problem has many aspects. It means that you are being blocked by long-standing habits which lead you to keep repeating the past, instead of making a new start. It means that you are out of touch with your feelings, and are living your life in terms of other people's expectations rather than your own. And it means you are letting others determine the goals you pursue and how far you can go in pursuing them. This is clearly responsible for much of the distress you describe and the impression you have that you are not in touch with your true self.

In addition, you haven't learned to concentrate on your strengths or to focus on a critical target while blocking out negative thoughts. This makes decisions very difficult for you. Most important of all, you are deceiving everyone (yourself included) by covering up the way you are feeling. You act as if you have it all together when in fact you don't feel together at all. This cover-up, while it seems to work on the surface, is actually tearing you up inside, making it impossible for you to acknowledge your dreams or allow yourself to be the person you want to be.

All of this is happening to you in a very difficult period of your life, one in which you are being brought face to face with demands and realities for which you have not been properly prepared. Your actions have new, unexpected results. You are encountering distrust and doubt. You don't know whom or what to believe. Your idols have suddenly turned out to have clay feet. You feel you don't have the skills to make critical judgments. As a result, you feel blue most of the time.

As I hope this letter has helped you see, one of the major causes of adolescent depression is the entertaining of unrealistic expectations. You may never have had to face failure, defeat or frustration before. You may never have learned to come from behind. And so your expectations may be unduly high, while you just haven't acquired the basic skills needed for adulthood.

You can achieve greater success, though. You're not doomed to be forever fixed in the illusory world of fantasy, powerlessness and dreams. But in order to get out of that world, you have to allow yourself first to experience feelings of discomfort, and then to ride them out. It takes effort, but the more you try, the more you will discover the enormous capacity you have to handle whatever life throws at you.

One of the great challenges of adolescence is the discovery and mastery of powerful emotional forces within yourself. Learning to accept your feelings—especially the uncomfortable ones—means you will soon be learning that feelings can't hurt you and that ultimately they don't last very long. As you try new things, furthermore, you will begin to feel less anxious, more comfortable about yourself, even amazed at how easy most "impossible" goals can be—if you change your attitude toward them.

But it's you, and nobody else, who is responsible for the feelings that you experience and how you handle them. You've seen how you can learn to condition yourself to deal with a range of experiences by mastering your inner responses. I'd urge you to practice the techniques for doing this, because ultimately it's much more useful than learning to cope with individual bad situations themselves. Get your mind working for you, and the matter will follow in short order.

You can also learn what to change about yourself by seeing what you do to create those external problems. Knowing how your own behavior triggers negative responses in others is a start toward seeing yourself as part of a wide, and manageable, communications system.

You probably already know that it's time for you to leave the fantasy world of childhood and enter the more difficult, and more interesting, world of adults. I hope my letter will stimulate you to do that by encouraging you to 1) express your feelings, 2) stop blaming others for your distress, 3) make fewer demands on others, 4) reduce the deceptiveness and defensiveness in your relationships, and 5) listen to the undertones of communication.

You are at a crossroads in your life. It is not the first. Nor will it be the last. Whatever mistakes you make in the coming years can be corrected. Moreover, the sooner you begin to rechart your course, the smoother that course will be. You can change the problems you encounter, but not by changing the world. You can only do it by changing your own way of thinking.

Nobody else can do this for you. It's your hand, as always, on the wheel. I have faith in you and know that you will be able to steer your own course.

If you have any questions or comments please don't hesitate to write to me. I'll try to get back to you as soon as I can.

With all my best wishes,

Sincerely,

Ari Kiev, M.D.